PREHISTORIC
BRITAIN

PREHISTORIC BRITAIN

ORKNEY IS. | **SHETLAND IS.**

SKARA BRAE

CLICKHIMIN

TO A SMALLER SCALE

Sites & Monuments mentioned in the text:

△ SACRED SITES
○ HILL FORTS
⌂ BARROWS
● SETTLEMENTS
◆ VARIOUS
---- TRACKWAYS

CAIRNPAPPLE

△ KESWICK
● GREAT LANGDALE

STAR CARR

FOLKTON

ANGLESEY

△ ARBOR LOW

● CRAIG LWYD   ▲ MOLD

ISNETTISHAM

PETERBOROUGH ●

GRIMES GRAVES

WEST HARLING

BOTTISHAM ●

CAMULODUNUM

HITCHIN
BELAS KNAP ▲   WHEATHAMSTEAD   CLACTON

PRESCELLY MTS.   VERULAMIUM

● BIRDLIP

TINKINSWOOD   WINDMILL HILL   HOUNSLOW

WEST KENNET   △ AVEBURY   TEDDINGTON   ● AYLESFORD
SWANSCOMBE
ALL CANNINGS CROSS   ● WOODHENGE

GLASTONBURY   △ STONEHENGE

● LITTLE WOODBURY

POLDEN HILL ●   CISSBURY   EASTBOURNE

MAIDEN CASTLE

RILLATON

SCALE
20 10 0   20   40   60   80   100
MILES

PREHISTORIC BRITAIN

TEXT BY BARBARA GREEN

DRAWINGS BY ALAN SORRELL

LUTTERWORTH PRESS · LONDON

First Published 1968
Second Impression 1969
Third Impression 1971
TEXT COPYRIGHT © 1968 BARBARA GREEN
DRAWINGS COPYRIGHT © 1968 ALAN SORRELL

In the same series:
ROMAN BRITAIN
Text by Aileen Fox, Drawings by Alan Sorrell

SAXON ENGLAND
Text by John Hamilton, Drawings by Alan Sorrell

NORMAN BRITAIN
Text by Henry Loyn, Drawings by Alan Sorrell

ACKNOWLEDGEMENTS

The jacket drawing is the property of the Ministry of Public Building and Works, and is reproduced with their permission. It is Crown Copyright. The drawings on pages 11 and 45 are based on others by Alan Sorrell published in the *Illustrated London News*, and are reproduced by courtesy of the Editor. Mr. Sorrell wishes to thank Mr. D. G. Macleod, M.A., of Prittlewell Priory Museum, for valuable assistance; the British Museum, for permission to include various drawings based on guide-book illustrations; the National Museum of Wales, for permission to include drawings of the long barrow burial at Tinkinswood, and of the " collared " urn, based on drawings by Mr. Sorrell which are their property; Mrs. E. M. Clifford, for the Birdlip Mirror; Dr. P. Jacobsthal, F.S.A., for the Hounslow boar and the Polden Hill harness mount; and Professor R. Atkinson, for permission to base a drawing on his original bluestone route map.

ISBN 0 7188 0781 2

PRINTED IN GREAT BRITAIN
BY FLETCHER AND SON LTD, NORWICH

CONTENTS

The jacket picture shows Stonehenge in its final state of 1400 B.C. The half-title page drawing is of Kit's Coty House near Aylesford, Kent; the bronze figure of a boar on the title-page, first century B.C. or early first century A.D., is from Hounslow, Middlesex; the coin is an Iron Age gold stater, made in Britain, mid-first century B.C.: obverse and reverse.

SOME OTHER BOOKS
ABOUT PREHISTORIC BRITAIN

Other good general books to read after this one are: Jacquetta and Christopher Hawkes, *Prehistoric Britain* (Chatto and Windus, 5th Edition 1962), and Grahame Clark, *Prehistoric England* (Batsford paperback 1962). V. Gordon Childe, *Prehistoric Communities of the British Isles* (Chambers 1940) is still the best general advanced survey although parts of it are out of date. It is out of print, but is worth trying to obtain through a library. K. P. Oakley, *Man the Tool-Maker* (British Museum [Natural History] 5th Edition 1965) gives a good general survey of flint-working and the types of tools produced. Sonia Cole, *The Neolithic Revolution* (British Museum [Natural History] 3rd Edition 1965) gives a good survey of the early history of farming, the crops grown and the types of animals kept. Good illustrations of Neolithic, Bronze Age and Iron Age pottery and metalwork can be found in *Later Prehistoric Antiquities of the British Isles* (British Museum [revised edition in production]).

Many other books on Prehistoric Britain can be found in your public library.

The Ordnance Survey have published maps which show the position of many important prehistoric sites. *Ancient Britain* (Revised Editions, South Sheet 1964 and North Sheet 1964) show visible antiquities up to 1066. *The Map of Southern Britain in the Iron Age* (1962) shows also the important sites and in the introduction gives a general survey of the period. Brief descriptions of these prehistoric sites are given in Nicholas Thomas, *A Guide to Prehistoric England* (Batsford 1960), and R. W. Feacham, *A Guide to Prehistoric Scotland* (Batsford 1963).

Further information can be found at your local museum.

1. *Straight-tusked elephants and rhinoceros—two of the wild animals which lived in southern Britain about 300,000 years ago. The climate of Britain at this time was much warmer than it is today.*

HUNTERS AND FISHERS (about 300000 B.C.—3500 B.C.)

WHEN Man first evolved he knew nothing about farming or the working of metals. He lived by hunting wild animals and by collecting fruits and berries and small creatures. His earliest tools and weapons were made of wood and stone. At first he picked up from the ground stones of the right shape and size, used them for the job in hand and then threw them away. Usually it is impossible to identify those used in this way. Later he learnt to trim stones to certain shapes and to obtain a sharp cutting edge by

2. *A Palaeolithic family group in a temporary encampment.   Two of the men are making flint hand-axes, while a third is finishing a wooden spear.*

knocking off flakes with another stone. It is these first, crudely-shaped tools which provide the earliest evidence for Man living in Britain.

These first tools, belonging to Old Stone Age or Palaeolithic man, are often found in gravel deposits which geologists have dated to about a quarter of a million years old. They were laid down during the Pleistocene period or Great Ice Age. Despite the name, Britain was not permanently covered with ice at this time. The fossil remains of animals and plants show that at least three times between 500,000 and 12,000 years ago the climate of Britain was much warmer than it is today.   The first certain tools come from the second

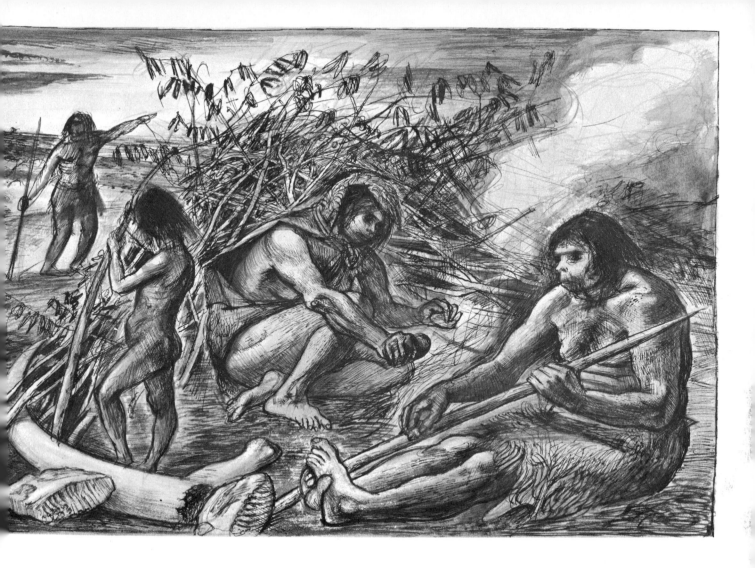

of these warm periods or Interglacials, when the straight-tusked elephant, much larger than the largest modern elephant, bison, wild horse, rhinoceros and many types of deer roamed over parts of Britain. In the second Interglacial, hippopotamus and lion can be added to the list.

Life was very difficult for human beings at this time. The grazing animals constantly changed their feeding grounds and the hunters had perforce to follow if they were to find food. From the study of modern primitive hunting tribes it seems likely that Palaeolithic man lived in family groups, probably of never more than fifty people at any time. The men would have hunted the big game, while the women and children collected wild plants, small animals and eggs.

Hunting must have been a dangerous business when hunters had only wooden spears, the tips of which were hardened by placing them in a fire, and stone tools carried in the hand. The hunters probably lay in wait beside a water-hole, waiting for an unsuspecting deer to come to drink, or they dug pits, which they covered with branches, in a game-trail.

Flint was the favourite stone used for these early tools, as it could be easily trimmed into shape, and given a sharp cutting edge.

The first stage in tool-making was to remove flakes from a large flint nodule by hitting it with another piece of flint known as a hammer-stone. The blows were not haphazard, but were done carefully and with a knowledge of how flint fractures. Further trimming was carried out by removing smaller flakes with a piece of wood or bone. This method produced a core tool. Some groups of people produced mainly core tools, only occasionally trimming the waste flakes into knives or scrapers for cleaning skins. The commonest core tool of the early part of the Palaeolithic period is the hand-axe. This was a general-purpose tool and was never hafted. Other groups of people made their tools from the

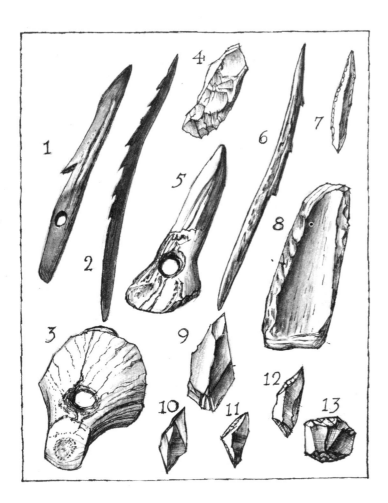

3. Bone and flint objects from a Mesolithic site at Star Carr: 1. Harpoon head made from red deer antler; 2. Barbed point of red deer antler, possibly a spearhead; 3. Mattock-head made from elk antler, perhaps used for grubbing up roots; 4. Flint adze or axe; 5. Mattock-head made from elk antler with an attached piece of bone; 6. Barbed point of red deer antler, possibly a spearhead; 7. Flint awl; 8. Leather-working tool of auroch's bone; 9. Flint burin used for working antler and bone; 10, 11, 12. Flint microliths used as arrowheads; 13. Double-ended flint scraper.

4. *Star Carr, Yorkshire.   A temporary camp of a group of Mesolithic hunters and fishers at the edge of a lake.   Bones of wild animals, killed in the chase, littered the site.   Many pieces were worked into tools and weapons.   The animals included red deer, elk and aurochs (wild ox).*

detached flakes and discarded the cores.   As Man gained greater skill in flint-knapping he found it possible to produce a greater variety of more efficient tools.

We know very little about Palaeolithic people, mainly for two reasons.   They had few possessions to leave behind them, and much of what they did leave, with the exception of their tough flint tools, was destroyed or covered up by later glaciations.

When the temperature dropped and glaciers began to move south over the country, the

5. A Mesolithic hunter stalking deer. He wears a cap made from the antlers and upper part of the skull of a red deer. This was worn to enable the hunter to creep close to his prey without frightening the animals. Red Indians used to stalk antelope in the same way.

wild animals on which the hunters lived also moved south. The hunters followed the animals. Britain was still connected to the Continent, so there was no barrier to this movement. It was only during the Last Glaciation that Man managed to live in southern Britain. This time the ice did not move as far south as before, and certain wild animals such as the woolly rhinoceros, the mammoth and the reindeer managed to feed on the sparse tundra vegetation.

These provided food for a few hardy hunters.

As the ice retreated north for the last time the temperature rose, and tundra plants, such as dwarf willow and dwarf birch, were replaced by birch, then pine, forests. These in their turn were replaced by forests of oak, elm and beech. New people came to Britain with new skills developed to deal with a changed environment. These are known as the Mesolithic or Middle Stone Age people. It is possible to identify different groups of flint implements of this period, each group suitable for a different environment. The flint tools found on the light, sandy soils, where there would have been few trees, are different from those found on heavier soils where there was forest. The flint tools of the forest-dwellers included small axes suitable for felling trees.

Though the Mesolithic people were more advanced technically than the Palaeolithic people, they still lived by hunting and fishing. From finds made on a temporary camping site at Star Carr near Scarborough, which has been excavated, we have learned quite a lot about the way of life of these people. The camp was on a platform of brushwood, clay and stones, which had been built out over a reed swamp bordering a lake. They hunted wild animals of the forest such as red deer, elk, wild pig and roe deer. They shot water-fowl with bow and arrow, and fished in the lake with spears. These spears had wooden handles to which were attached prongs made from red deer antler. We know from other sites that Mesolithic people had fishing nets with bark floats and dug-out canoes, suitable for travelling on inland waterways, made by hollowing out tree trunks.

One of the most interesting groups of finds from Star Carr was a number of red deer skulls with the antlers still attached. Most of the bone had been cut away, leaving a cap. The bone was pierced in two places, probably for leather thongs. It is not known whether these were worn for some magical ceremony, or by hunters while stalking deer, to enable them to creep close to their quarry.

Scotland was first inhabited by Man during this period. The majority of the sites on which flints and other objects have been found are along the seacoast. Though these people certainly hunted red deer, they also found food on the shore or in the sea. Mounds of shells of limpets, oysters, whelks, mussels and winkles were gradually built up from the remains of their meals. The number of people living near the bleak Scottish coasts at this time was very few, less than in southern Britain.

8. (See page 15.) Section through a flint mine at Grime's Graves, Norfolk, showing how it was probably worked. A deep shaft was dug through the chalk until a band of particularly tough flint, now known as " floorstone ", was reached. At this level galleries were excavated radiating out from the bottom of the shaft, so that more flint could be extracted without shifting too much chalk. This flint was taken to the surface to be made into tools.

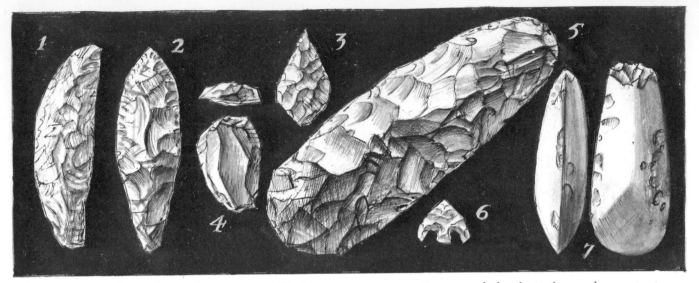

6. Neolithic flint implements: 1. Sickle for reaping grain; 2. Dagger made by the Beaker people; 3. Leaf-shaped arrowhead; 4. Scraper for cleaning skins; 5. Chipped axehead for felling trees; 6. Barbed and tanged arrowhead used by the Beaker people; 7. Polished axehead for felling trees.

8. Grime's Graves. See caption on page 13.

7. Neolithic bone and stone objects: 1. Chalk lamp used in the galleries of the flint mines at Grime's Graves, Norfolk; 2. Flint hammerstone, used in roughing-out flint implements; 3. Red deer antler pick used in flint mining for prising out blocks of chalk and flint; 4. Flint axe showing method of hafting; 5. Antler-comb, probably used in leather-working; 6. Chalk figurine depicting the goddess of fertility, found in Pit 15, Grime's Graves, Norfolk.

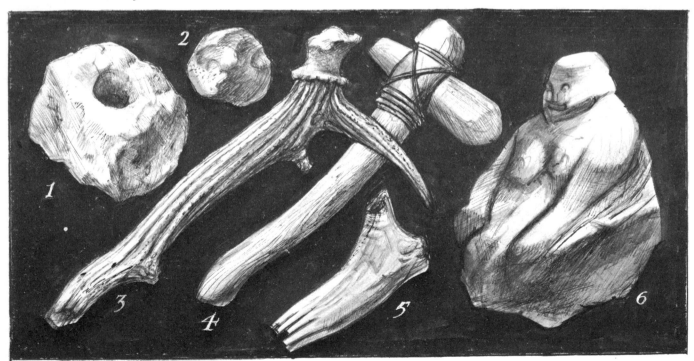

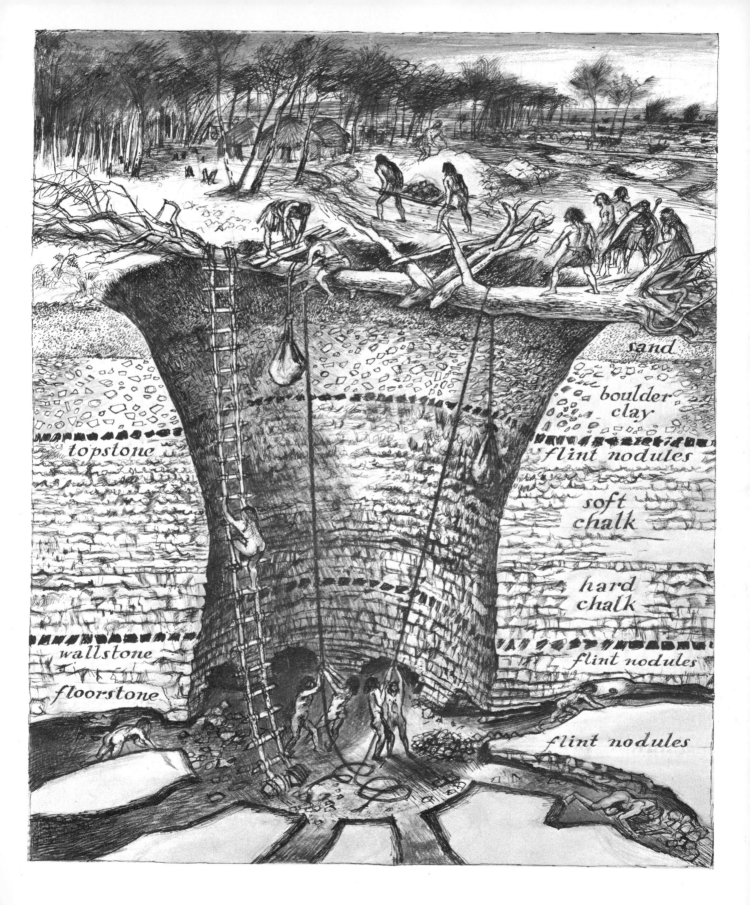

sand

boulder-
clay

flint nodules

topstone

soft
chalk

hard
chalk

wallstone

flint nodules

floorstone

flint nodules

THE FIRST FARMERS (about 3500 B.C. – 1500 B.C.)

While people lived by hunting and fishing in Britain, great changes were occurring in the Middle East. There, by 8000 B.C., people had learned to domesticate sheep and goats, to plant the seed of wild grasses near their huts, and to make pottery, by hand, out of clay. Gradually these new ideas spread to Europe.

However, it was not until about 3500 B.C. that the first farmers (the Neolithic or New Stone Age people) crossed the Channel to settle in southern Britain. They brought with them new types of flint tools, barley, sheep and goats and pottery vessels, mainly round-bottomed bowls. They settled first on the chalk lands and sandy areas, where the woodland could easily be cleared and the light soils easily tilled.

It was necessary to clear patches of woodland before the grain could be sown. For this they used polished stone and flint axes, set in wooden hafts. Modern experiments in Denmark have shown that these axes were efficient; trees 7 inches in diameter could be chopped down in 5 minutes. The ground was tilled by picking the soil with a flint or antler pick or with a wooden digging-stick. The grain was then scattered over the soil. The crop was reaped with flint sickles.

Cattle and pigs were kept, as well as the sheep and goats. Probably the wild cattle and pigs living in the forests were domesticated. Greater numbers of these animals were kept for they could continue to feed in the woods. Grass was available only in clearings for the sheep and goats. It was necessary constantly to clear fresh patches of woodland, for the light soils soon became exhausted. The grazing of the sheep and goats prevented the regrowth of trees, and gradually large areas of woodland were replaced by tracts of grassland.

Many of the tree-felling axes were made of flint picked up from the surface, but they tended to shatter. Early on in the Neolithic period much tougher axes began to be made of hard, fine-grained rocks. These were our first industrial products, being made at a number of factory sites in western and northern Britain. Geologists have studied a large number of these stone axes and have so far identified eighteen factory sites in Cornwall, Wales, the Lake District and Teesdale.

9. *Neolithic hut at Skara Brae, Orkney Islands. This is one of a group of single-roomed, stone-built huts. There was a central hearth where peat was burned. Along two walls were stone box-beds, which probably had heather mattresses. At one end, opposite the doorway, was a stone dresser. The roof, which was perhaps of turves laid over a framework of timber or whale bones, has been removed to show the interior.*

10. *Burial ceremony at Tinkinswood, Glamorgan, in a chambered long barrow. Dead bodies were placed in the burial chamber of this Neolithic burial mound over a number of years. When someone died, the stone blocking the entrance was removed and the body placed inside. Elaborate ceremonies took place near the entrance to the tomb.*

The products of these factories were traded to farmers all over southern Britain.

Flint occurs in bands in chalk, and certain bands are very tough. About 2000 B.C. large-scale mining began for this tough flint. A number of sites have been found in southern Britain, the most famous of which is at Grime's Graves in Norfolk. Here excavations have shown that the Neolithic miners worked some 34 acres for a particular

band of flint. Some of the mining was open-cast, but 366 deep shafts were sunk into the chalk in the search for this flint band. These shafts, which vary from 15 to 40 feet in depth, were dug with the most primitive tools—picks made of red deer antlers, shovels from ox shoulder blades, and flint axes. When the miners reached the flint layer, they dug tunnels radiating out from the bottom of the shaft, so that the maximum flint could be removed for the minimum effort. Two of these shafts have been left open after archaeological excavation, and it is possible to crawl round the tunnels.

Little is known of the houses of the Neolithic farmers of southern and eastern Britain.

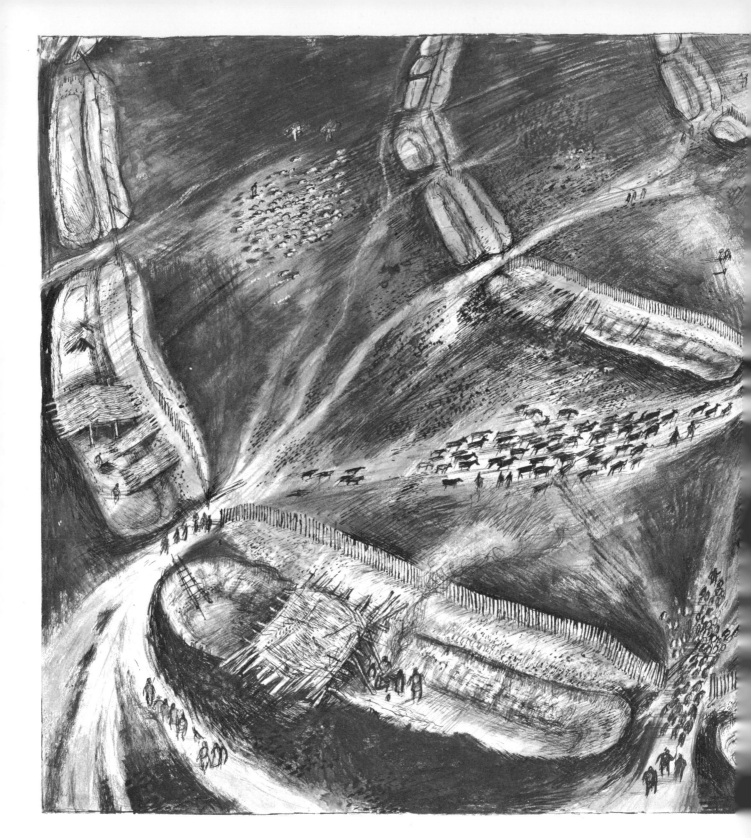

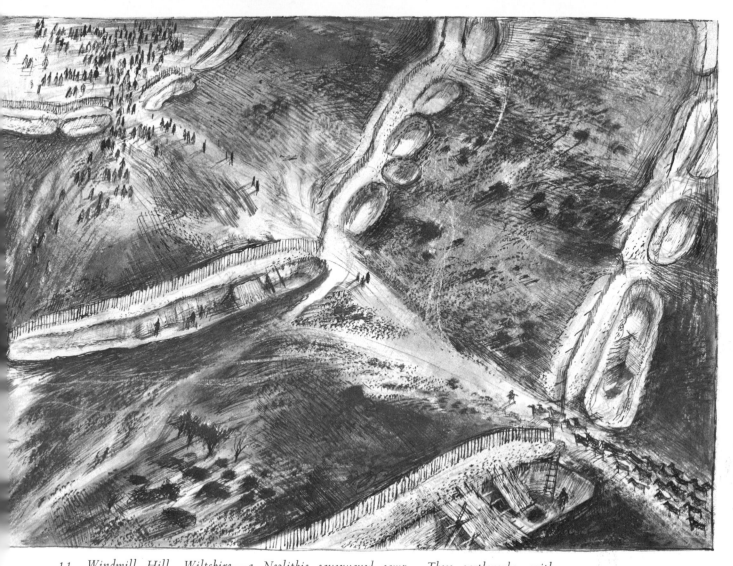

11. *Windmill Hill, Wiltshire—a Neolithic causewayed camp. These earthworks, with usually two or three concentric rings of banks and ditches, broken at intervals with causeways, are found in southern England. They were probably tribal centres, where people met for tribal ceremonies and the exchange of seed corn and stock.*

They were probably of timber and turf, and little survives when they are excavated. In the Highland areas of western and northern Britain stone was used. Rectangular and round huts were built. The best preserved can be seen at Skara Brae in the Orkney Islands. Here a group of at least eight huts were built, partly underground. Each house was a single room linked to others by tunnels. The rooms were rectangular, and in the centre of each was a hearth for a peat fire. Along the side walls, beds of heather were

12. *The bluestones used in building the second temple at Stonehenge were carried by raft along the South Wales coast. Transporting these great blocks by water was much easier than dragging them overland.*

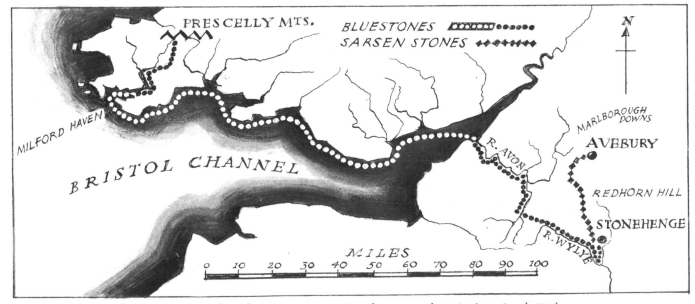

12a. *The great stones used in the construction of Stonehenge were brought from South Wales (bluestones) and Marlborough Downs (sarsens).*

enclosed by stone slabs over which were draped skin canopies to keep the draughts out. Above each bed a small hole in the wall contained the occupant's private possessions. On the rear wall was a stone dresser.

More is known of the houses of the dead. Elaborate tombs, long barrows, were constructed to contain the dead. In southern and eastern England the tombs were made of earth or chalk rubble, usually higher and broader at one end and with shallow ditches on either side. A number of people were buried together beneath these mounds. Excavations have shown that often the first structure was a timber building, in which the dead bodies were placed. When a number of bodies had been laid there, sometimes as many as fifty, the mound was raised over the mortuary house, completely concealing it. In Wiltshire, East Anglia and the north of England, the bodies were cremated before the barrow was built.

13.   The second temple at Stonehenge was built between about 1650 and 1500 B.C.   A double circle of bluestones was set up inside the bank and ditch of the first temple on the site. This bank can be seen beyond the stone circle.

14. *The sarsen blocks used for building the third temple at Stonehenge had to be moved over-land. They were probably lashed to sledges running on rollers. At least 100 men were needed to pull each sledge.*

In western and northern Britain the long barrows take the form of elaborate stone chambers. These also were communal burial places. When someone died, the great stone covering the entrance was rolled aside and the body placed carefully in the chamber. Ceremonies were held at the time of the burial, but little is known of the rites.

Though little is known of the gods worshipped by the Neolithic people, a discovery made in the flint mines at Grime's Graves, Norfolk, shows that there was a fertility cult. At the bottom of the shaft of Pit 15 archaeologists found a crude altar made from chalk blocks. On the altar lay seven red deer antler picks. On a ledge near by stood a chalk figurine of a pregnant woman. There was very little of the tough flint in this pit, and it has been suggested that this group was an offering to the goddess of fertility, so that there would be plenty of the flint in the next pit the miners dug.

A number of sacred sites of the Neolithic period have been recognised in different parts of Britain. The most famous is Stonehenge on Salisbury Plain. This temple was rebuilt several times, for the last time in the following Early Bronze Age. The first temple here, constructed about 1800 B.C., was very simple. It took the form of a pennanular earthen bank with a shallow external ditch. Inside the bank, and dug close to it, was a circle of 56 pits. At the entrance stood two great upright stones. The ceremonies took place inside the circle, while the congregation watched from the bank.

The second temple was built by a group of people who had emigrated to Britain from the Low Countries about 2000 B.C. These are called the Beaker people from their characteristic pottery vessels. They brought with them the earliest metal tools made of copper, and many new customs. They buried their dead, singly, beneath round barrows, often placing beside the body grave goods intended for use in the next world.

This Beaker temple at Stonehenge was built inside the earthen bank at the end of the

Neolithic period, between about 1650 and 1500 B.C. Some 60 large stones, each weighing up to one and a half tons, were brought to the site and set up in a double circle. These stones, known as the bluestones, were brought some 240 miles from the Prescelly Mountains in South Wales, a tremendous feat. They were probably brought by boat along the South Wales coast, across the Bristol Channel, along the rivers Avon and Frome, Wylye and Salisbury Avon. The journey on land would thus be short.

The stones were probably then moved on sledges dragged on wooden rollers by teams of men.

THE FIRST METAL-WORKERS (about 1500 B.C.–600 B.C.)

At some time between 2000 and 1500 B.C. Beaker people and colonists from the Iberian Peninsula settled in Ireland and began to work there the abundant supplies of copper ores. The first metal tools were made of copper, but smiths soon learnt that by adding a little tin to the copper it was possible to make a much tougher metal—bronze. The early metal tools are simple in form and relatively rare, but as the smiths gradually learnt new skills they were able to produce a greater variety of metal objects in more complicated shapes. At first only the wealthy could afford these new efficient tools, but as time went on other members of the community were able to acquire them.

The commonest tool of the Bronze Age was the axe, used for tree-felling and by the

16. *In the Early Bronze Age a third temple was built at Stonehenge. Great blocks of sarsen were set up, the outer circle being capped with stone lintels. These lintels were raised gradually on stacked timbers until the tops of the upright stones were reached. The lintels were then eased on to the uprights.*

15.   *Raising the upright sarsens at Stonehenge.   A pit was dug for each stone with one side vertical and the opposite side a sloping ramp.   The stone was levered up off the sledge until its base dropped into the hole.   It was then hauled upright and packed in position with stones.*

carpenters for wood-working.   The earliest axes were flat and liable to slip in their wooden hafts.   Before the end of the Early Bronze Age, about 1400 B.C., smiths had learnt to cast axes with flanges along the sides of the upper part of the axe which prevented them slipping sideways in the haft.   In the Middle Bronze Age (about 1400 to 1000 B.C.) a further improvement was the addition of a horizontal ridge joining the side flanges; this type of axe is known as the palstave.   In the Late Bronze Age (about 1000 to 600 B.C.) the smiths developed the socketed axe.   At this time many other carpenter's tools were produced in bronze, such as gouges, bits and chisels.   Metal weapons improved too.   The daggers, spears and knives, produced from the Early Bronze Age, were supplemented in the Middle Bronze Age by rapiers.   In the Late Bronze Age the heavy cutting sword replaced the lighter rapier.   Bronze shields are also known, made of thin sheet metal which could be easily hacked to pieces with a heavy sword.   These shields were probably used only for ceremonial purposes; in war a warrior would have carried a heavy wooden or leather shield, such as have been found in peat bogs.   Buckets and cauldrons of sheet bronze, horse harness fittings and jewellery all testify to the increasing skill of the smiths.

17.   The completed third temple at Stonehenge, about 1400 B.C.   The bluestones of the second temple had been removed when the sarsens were set up.   The bluestones were re-erected inside the sarsen circle.

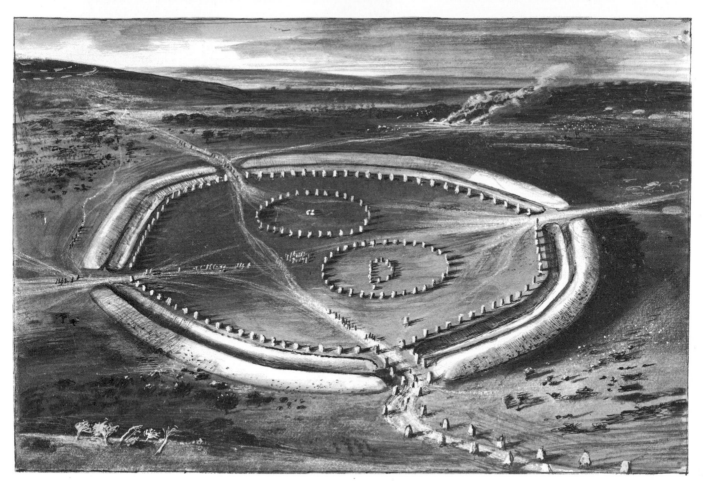

18. *Avebury, Wiltshire. This Late Neolithic temple is much larger than Stonehenge. The circular earth bank, which encloses several stone circles, is over 1300 feet in diameter. The stones used for the stone circles are of sarsen, as are the upright stones marking the processional way leading to the temple.*

At first metal tools were produced in Ireland and Scotland where supplies of ores were easily available; the tin was brought from Cornwall. Copper ores were broken up and heated with charcoal in a clay-lined bowl furnace dug into the ground. The temperature in the furnace was raised to 1100° C., so that the copper separated from the ore and ran to the bottom of the furnace where it formed a "metal-cake". This was removed when the furnace cooled. Tin ores were smelted in a similar way. Pieces of copper and tin "cake" were melted in a crucible. The molten metal was poured into a mould, covered and left to cool. The bronze object was taken from the mould, the rough edges trimmed and then it was polished. Sometimes pieces were decorated. If a cutting edge was needed, the implement had to be sharpened.

19. *Bronze Age burial mounds and grave goods. Round barrows are the commonest visible prehistoric monuments in Britain. A number of different types were constructed, some of which can be seen in the background. Many different types of grave goods were placed with the dead in these burial mounds. Pottery vessels of different forms are among the commonest objects found in the excavation of these mounds; four types are shown here. Occasionally cups of shale, amber and even gold, like that from Rillaton, Devon, were buried. Other gold ornaments found with burials include small plaques and coverings for buttons (in centre).*

Gradually, as more and more people acquired metal objects, supplies of bronze became available in other parts of Britain in the form of broken and obsolete tools and weapons. Metalsmiths began to travel round, buying up the old objects and melting them down to cast new ones. If there were insufficient customers in an area the smith would bury any remaining scrap metal in a hole in the ground, presumably intending to use it next time he came there. Sometimes he never returned, for these deposits are found from time to time today, while digging or ploughing the land.

Jewellery for men and women was made from bronze and, for the very wealthy, from gold. The gold was found in Ireland, and made there into jewellery such as ear-rings, bracelets, neck torcs and also mountings for dagger hilts. These pieces were traded to many parts of Britain and also to the Continent; some have been found in Mycenean graves in Greece. The trade route from Ireland to Europe lay across Salisbury Plain, and in the Early Bronze Age was controlled by the chieftains living there. The rich objects buried with these Wessex chieftains illustrate their power and wealth. They were probably responsible for the final rebuilding of Stonehenge in the form we know it today.

The bluestones set up by the Beaker people were removed. Great blocks of sarsen, a

20. *A Bronze Age metalsmith casting bronze implements. Bronze ingots or scrap metal were melted in a crucible. The smith is seen pouring molten metal into a mould. This was then covered and left to cool. The bronze object was then removed from the mould, trimmed, sharpened if necessary and polished.*

sandstone found on the surface of Marlborough Downs to the north of Salisbury Plain, were dragged to the site. There they were carefully worked. A circle of upright stones was set up, and on them were laid stone lintels. Stone pegs had been carved on the uprights, while cup-shaped hollows in the lintels fitted over these pegs. Inside this circle the builders set up five trilithons, each of two great upright stones with a third laid across the top. The bluestones were finally erected inside the sarsen settings.

This temple is unique in Europe. Carvings of Mycenean daggers on some of the sarsens have led some archaeologists to suggest that Greek masons may have helped in the building of this great monument. This idea is not impossible, for there was contact with the Continent throughout the Bronze Age. British smiths learnt new skills from Continental smiths, British bronzes have been found in Europe and Continental bronzes in Britain, and from British graves have come blue glass beads made in the Eastern Mediterranean.

Many imported luxuries have been found with burials. In the Early Bronze Age the commonest burial custom was inhumation beneath a round barrow, though cremation was also practised. Bronze Age barrows are among the commonest field monuments in Britain, though many have been, or are being, destroyed by ploughing. These barrows were carefully constructed tombs, sometimes with timber structures hidden within the mound. In some areas the mounds were of chalk, gravel or soil; where stone was available elaborate cairns were made.

The richest grave goods come from the burials of the Wessex chieftains. They are found mainly on Salisbury Plain, but burials belonging to this group have been found as far north as Norfolk. The grave goods include bronze axes and daggers, some with gold-decorated hilts, stone maceheads (probably a symbol of rank), amber, jet and blue glass beads, stone weapons and flint arrowheads. Small, elaborately decorated vessels were also sometimes placed in graves. The majority of Bronze Age burials contain few grave goods except for pottery vessels.

In the Middle and Late Bronze Age the normal burial rite was cremation. The ashes were interred in or under large urns either under a new mound or in existing barrows. In parts of southern Britain in the Late Bronze Age, cremation urns were placed in flat cemeteries.

Far less is known about the daily life of the Bronze Age people than about their burial customs and their metal-work.   In the Early Bronze Age people were mainly pastoralists, who moved around with their flocks and herds seeking new pasture.   They grew a little grain.   By the beginning of the Middle Bronze Age in southern Britain a simple scratch plough, drawn by a pair of oxen, had been introduced.   This enabled farmers to cultivate larger areas of land than had been possible with simple hand tools.   Small rectangular fields were ploughed first one way, then again at right-angles.   Fields were now manured, so that it was no longer necessary to move to fresh plots every few years.   From the few excavations which have so far been carried out on Middle and Late Bronze Age farms in southern Britain, it seems that families lived in isolated farmsteads.   Groups of round

21.   Storing grain.   After the grain crop was harvested it was threshed and then, after drying, poured into storage pits which were sometimes lined with wickerwork.   This method of storage is known from the Neolithic throughout the rest of the prehistoric period.

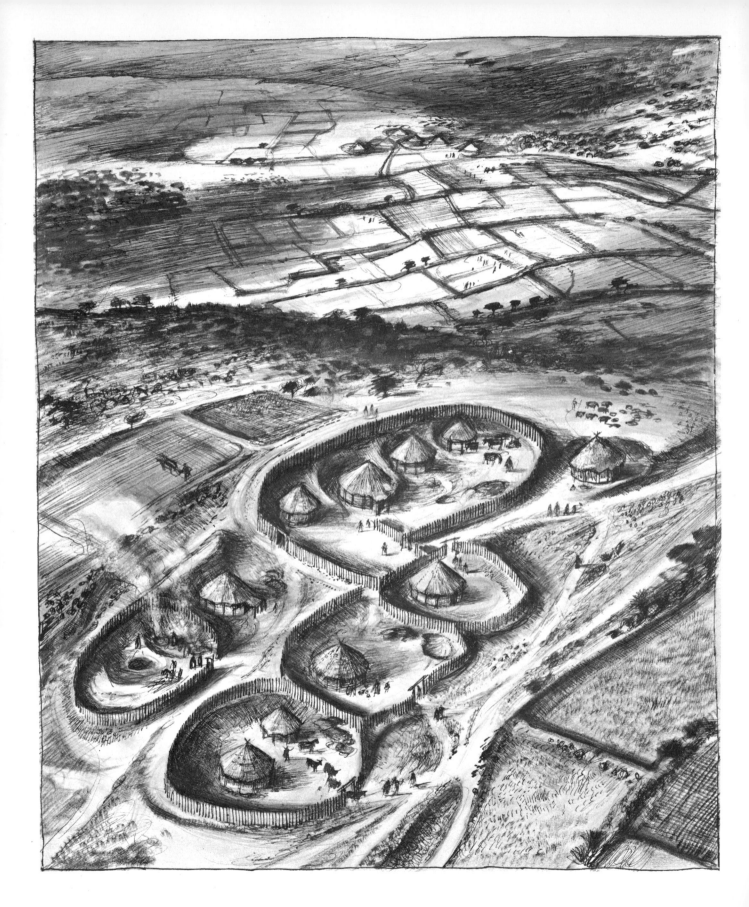

23. *Weaving on an upright loom. Both woollen and linen fabrics were woven; often these were dyed bright colours.*

22. *A downland farm of the Bronze Age. Bronze Age farmers practised mixed farming in southern Britain. Their small rectangular fields (in the background) were cultivated with a simple scratch plough. Farmers and their families lived in isolated farmsteads. The round huts, protected by wooden stockades, served a number of different purposes. Some were dwelling-houses, while others were used for animals or for storage.*

huts, with walls of wattle-and-daub and thatched roofs, were used for sleeping in, and as barns and workshops and shelters for animals.

In the hilly areas of western and northern Britain there is little evidence of this type of farming. Here stock-rearing seems to have been more important than corn-growing, though some grain was produced.

Clay weights from vertical looms and textile impressions in pottery indicate that the weaving of cloth began in Britain during the Bronze Age. No costume has been found in this country, but some pieces found in Danish burials give us, perhaps, some idea of what British Bronze Age people wore. A man was dressed in a loin cloth, which fell from under his arms to his knees. Over his shoulders was a cloak, on his feet were leather shoes and on his head a round brimless cap. His hair was short and he was clean-shaven. A woman wore a woollen blouse, with sleeves to the elbow, over a skirt. This was either long or very short. The latter was made of woollen cords, attached at top and bottom to woollen strips. Women had long hair, worn either loose or elaborately styled over a pad and covered with a horse-hair net.

THE WARRIOR SOCIETY (about 600 B.C. – A.D. 43)

On many hills in Britain can still be seen the great earthen banks and ditches of Iron Age hillforts. Nowadays it is quite easy to walk over the crumbled ramparts into the central area defended by these banks. But when these forts were first constructed, the ramparts and steep-sided ditches provided formidable obstacles to attackers. A wooden palisade or stone wall usually protected the defenders standing on the inner rampart as they hurled iron-tipped spears and sling stones at their opponents.

These forts vary very much in size. The earthworks of the smallest and earliest, usually only a single bank and ditch, enclose areas of only a few acres. The largest, with several lines of ramparts, can cover well over a hundred acres. Not all the forts were on hill tops. Sometimes a spur of high land with steep drops on most sides was fortified by the construction of banks and ditches across the neck of the spur. The ramparts of some forts were earthen banks with palisades on top, but others were more complex. Some-times the ramparts were laced with timber, while others were revetted in front with wood or stone. In some areas, the ramparts were constructed of dry-stone walling. The entrances to these forts were always the weak point in the defences. Wooden gates and towers protected the breaks in the ramparts, and further protection was sometimes given by an elaborate arrangement of curved banks and ditches.

It seems likely that the first forts were built by small groups of people under warrior leaders. There was probably great rivalry among neighbouring groups, and these forts provided a refuge at the time of an attack; there is no evidence that people lived permanently in them. In the larger forts, constructed later in the Iron Age, villages gradually grew up. As the population increased, family groups banded together into tribes. A warrior aristocracy arose to rule over the farmers and craftsmen. From coins and Roman histories

24. *Throughout the Bronze Age there was trade between Britain and the continent of Europe. Ships crossed the Channel bringing goods to be exchanged for other products in Britain, as there was no money at that time.*

25. *Iron Age metalwork and pottery: 1. Bronze mask from Welwyn, Hertfordshire. This was originally mounted in a bowl; 2. Gold neck torc from Snettisham, Norfolk; 3. Bronze harness mount decorated with red enamel from Polden Hill, Somerset; 4. Bronze handle-swivel from a wooden bucket found at Aylesford, Kent; 5. Pottery bowl from Glastonbury, Somerset. The decoration is similar to that found on metal objects; 6. Pottery jar decorated on the rim with finger-tipping found at Walthamstow, Essex. This is a common Early Iron Age type of vessel; 7. Belgic pedestal urn from Hitchin, Hertfordshire.*

we know the names of many of these British tribes and the areas they controlled at the time of the Roman Conquest.

Prowess in war was much admired, and the warrior chieftains were richly dressed. A chieftain dressed for war was a gay figure, clad in a brightly coloured tunic, a striped cloak pinned at the shoulder with a bronze brooch, a gleaming bronze helmet on his head, an iron sword in a decorated scabbard at his side, and on his left arm an elaborately decorated bronze shield.   He wore bracelets on his arms and sometimes a gold or bronze torc around his neck.

The metal-workers of the Iron Age were skilled craftsmen.   They produced iron tools for the farmer and carpenter, iron swords for the warrior, bronze cauldrons, harness fittings, shields and helmets, mirrors and brooches.   The most skilled were artists who decorated bronze and gold with beautiful abstract designs, and who sometimes further embellished their work with brilliant red enamel.

The majority of the population throughout the Iron Age, despite their gradual organisation into tribal units, continued to farm in the same way as had their Bronze Age

26.   *Iron Age farmstead at Little Woodbury, Wiltshire.   The circular farmhouse stood inside a compound surrounded by a wooden stockade.   Corn was dried on racks (to the right of the house); when dry it was threshed, then the grain was parched in an oven and stored in pits (behind the house).*

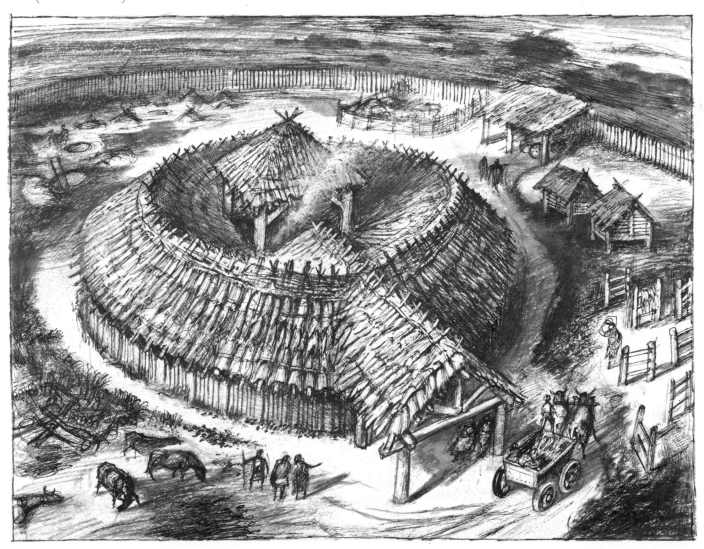

ancestors. In southern Britain many continued to live on isolated farmsteads in round huts, tilling the soil with ox-drawn scratch ploughs and herding cattle, sheep and pigs. Grain was still parched in clay ovens and stored in pits. Hay-making seems to have been introduced in this period, to provide winter feed for the animals.

In Somerset small villages have been found built, for defence, over marshy ground. The most famous of these is at Glastonbury. Here the builders constructed a platform in the marsh on which they built their houses. The water-logged soil has preserved many objects, such as wooden bowls and ladders, which add considerably to our knowledge of Iron Age domestic life, for such objects have usually disappeared on drier sites.

27. Building an Iron Age Stone fort in Scotland. The walls of these stone forts were laced with timber. Several have been found destroyed by fire. The intense heat given off by the burning timbers caused the stones to fuse. They are then known as vitrified forts.

28. Maiden Castle, Dorset, the most famous of the British Iron Age hillforts. The weak point in the defences of these forts was the entrance. An elaborate arrangement of curving banks and ditches was devised to protect this.

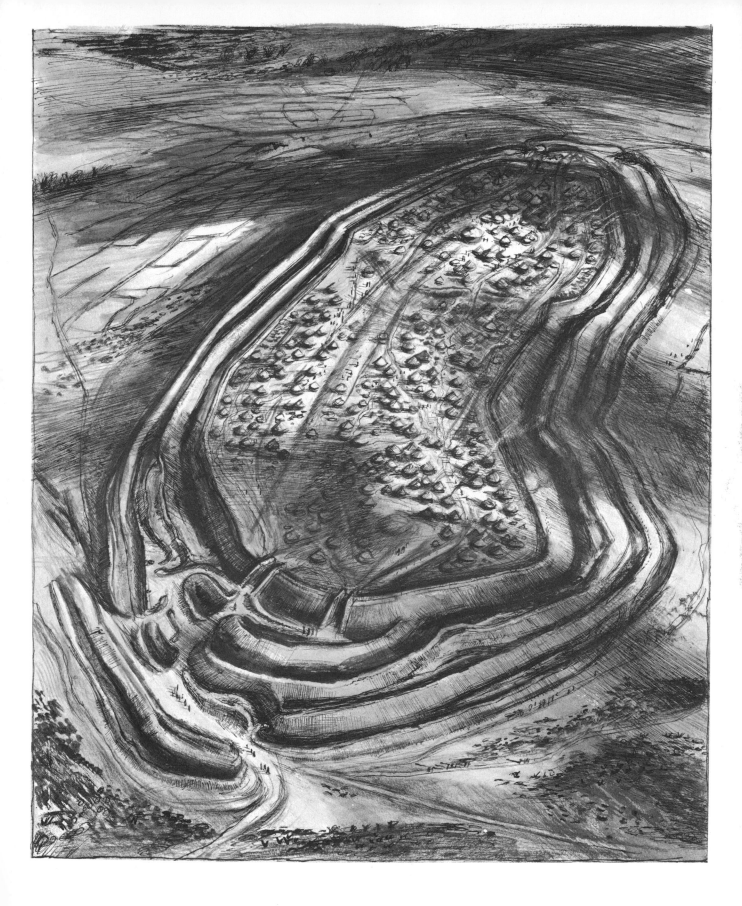

29. *An Iron Age warrior chieftain. These men loved bright colours and their trousers, tunics and cloaks were often dyed. In war they wore helmets and carried shields and were armed with swords and javelins. The soldiers behind are blowing war trumpets.*

In the wetter and hillier west and north the people were engaged mainly in cattle-rearing, growing only a little grain. It has been suggested the major tribe in northern England specialised in horse-rearing.

Large numbers of horses were needed during the Iron Age in Britain. Long after the custom had died out on the Continent, British warriors went to war in chariots. These were drawn by a pair of ponies, driven by a charioteer. Julius Caesar described the method of chariot warfare when he came to Britain in 55 and 54 B.C. The chariots were driven fast up and down in front of the enemy lines in an attempt to overawe him. There was a great deal of shouting and blowing of bronze trumpets to add to the effect. After a while the warriors leapt from their chariots to fight opponents in single combat. The chariot

30. *When Julius Caesar landed in Britain in 55 B.C. he was attacked by British tribesmen. Caesar described how they rode to war in chariots drawn by a pair of ponies. These chariots were driven up and down in front of the enemy troops in an attempt to frighten them.*

31.   An Iron Age village at Glastonbury, Somerset.   For defence, the village was built on an artificial island of earth, stone and timber on the edge of a shallow lake.   Further protection was provided by a wooden stockade.   Other settlements of this type are known in Somerset. Because of the dampness of the site wood and leather objects have been preserved.

waited near by so that the warrior could, if necessary, escape quickly. There is no evidence that scythes were ever attached to the wheels.

Throughout the Iron Age there was contact and trade with Europe. The idea of chariot warfare came from the Continent, as did the artistic styles so successfully used by British craftsmen to decorate their metalwork. The wealthy bought fine pottery, wine, metalwork and glassware produced in the Roman Empire.

The Britons exported cattle, grain, gold, cloth and slaves; these were prisoners taken in battle.

32. *A broch at Clickhimin, Shetland Islands. These fortified farmsteads are found in the north of Scotland. A stone tower, usually about 40 feet high, enclosed a central courtyard. Galleries in the thickness of the wall were reached by internal staircases. There was only one small entrance leading into the courtyard. A well or water-cistern has been found in many brochs, showing that the inhabitants could withstand sieges.*

33. *The conquest of the British. The Roman conquest of Britain started in A.D. 43, but it took many years to subdue the tribes of England and Wales. The tribes of Wales were led by Caratacus. They were defeated at a battle in Wales in A.D. 51.*

One of the most important introductions from the Continent, about 100 B.C., was coinage. In western Britain iron currency bars had been used in trading, but the new coinage was of gold. Many of the coins were based on earlier Greek coins. Later, silver coins were added to the currency. As coins began to be made in Britain, each tribe gradually developed its own distinctive designs. Many of the latest Iron Age coins bear the names of the tribal rulers.

Between 100 and 50 B.C. large numbers of a Continental group of people arrived in

Britain, known as the Belgae. In contrast to the British pottery, which the women still made by hand, the Belgic pottery was thrown on a wheel. Many of these elegant vessels have been found accompanying the cremated remains of the dead. Cremation was another custom in which the Belgae differed from the British tribes, who inhumed their dead.

The Belgae settled first near the south coast. They were as warlike as the other Iron Age peoples and apparently superior as warriors, for gradually they conquered some of the tribes already established in southern England. They constructed great tribal capitals, which were defended by long earthen banks and ditches. At the time of the Roman conquest, the most important capital was probably Camulodunum, just outside modern Colchester.

Though Julius Caesar brought large forces with him on his two expeditions to Britain in 55 and 54 B.C., and succeeded in defeating the British warriors in several battles, he withdrew to Gaul after subduing the Belgic centre at Wheathampstead. It was not until A.D. 43 that another and more powerful force gathered in Gaul and crossed the English Channel to land in Kent. This began the Roman conquest of Britain.

34. The Birdlip mirror.